HEGEL ON IDEALISM, KNOWLEDGE & REALITY

ISBN: 978-1-4717-0954-8

2012 COPYRIGHT © ANDREAS SOFRONIOU

HEGEL ON IDEALISM, KNOWLEDGE & REALITY

ISBN: 978-1-4717-0954-8

CONTENTS: PAGE:

CONCEPTUAL COMPREHENSION

It is believed that the subject of philosophy; being wise, offering advice, guidance and in general, counselling people in modern times has become a profession in its own right. With this in mind, this book hopes to address an important alternative in treating the homo-sapiens and his/her discomforts in living as an individual and in groups, whatever the choice may be.

The content of this book will still be of importance to the reader and without any compromising, a training tool for the practising philosopher. There is no doubt that this subject is deep and vast. Backed by recent social events and political debating, philosophy in its plentiful branches can only be helpful in preparing people to obtain an acceptable style of living and a harmonious mode of interacting with society.

The book is based on the historical established concepts and didactics of philosophers through the ages, from the Hellenic rhetorics, to recent European schools of ideas. All the teachings of philosophers and sophists explain the right of a person to live as a politis (citizen) in a near enough democratic state. The right to integrate and in doing so to live as an entity with his/her own attributes and behaviour within a society. In doing so, philosophers have debated the morals, norms, laws, beliefs, religions and logically enough what can

be an acceptable pattern of attitudes within the parameters of social tolerance.

Philosophers through the aeons have advised and counselled on the upbringing of children and offered guidance in establishing the right relationship between the child, the parents, and the state. More recently, analytical philosophies such as the neo-Freudian and Jungian schools established the methods of treating people, based on the classical idealism, with Socrates probably being the father of the method of question and answer. Sophocles, through his surviving tragedies, is certainly the major contributor to the psycho-analytical Oedipus and Electra complexes and perhaps the biggest influence on Freud and his successors.

Modern philosophical concepts have grown into such a vast amount of methodologies that people are often confused as to what they should follow.

Philosophy in general (just as much as all social branches of philosophy and political philosophy), maintains closer links with the constitution of the individual and groups of people living together, simply because a human being all along bears with himself/herself the philosophy of the environment they live in; the beliefs and the philosophy established through the ages. What a better way to treat a human being, other than the use of the logic as taught by the traditional philosopher

and as followed by the individual seeking assistance with the understanding of his/her nature?

Philosophical thinking and theories have been with us since the times of the olden. The logic expressed by philosophers can only assist in the understanding of human behaviour and in cases where necessary, the way in which philosophy can contribute to the treatment of the individual.

Put in an alternative way. A person carries his/her own philosophical ideals and talks of his/her own beliefs, rights, religion, norms, political and social philosophy. Further on, an individual (therapist, patient or client and reader) may follow the teachings of any one or more of the great philosophers. It can, therefore, be maintained that in such circumstances a client can be assisted by a therapeutic philosopher. A philosopher who, in turn, has an extended comprehension of the philosophical schools of ideas and how these teachings can help in counselling and treating a client.

If this book is to accomplish its purpose and be of real service to the citizen, mothers, fathers and the society of the future generation, it must be applicable and adaptable to people in all walks of life, simple and direct in its contents.

It is very easy to write for men and women already well advanced in the study of this subject and who have abundant means to supply the needs of social groups. But there are

others in less favourable circumstances, those who need instruction badly and any attempt to write on the philosophy of the adult and child must be broad enough to reach all who might be helped by such a book.

Many will understand the explanations which are given carefully and grasp quickly the subject which is treated at considerable length. These details are set forth so that no one who undertakes the reading of this book may fail to comprehend the thought intended and be benefited thereby.

The book is offered to all people; parents, teachers, leaders, therapists and to those who care about the future, the generations that will follow the present legacy. It is hoped that people in all walks of life will find the contents simple enough; a guide towards the understanding of the individual and his/her inter-relationship with the world.

There are a variety of ways in which philosophy counselling can be introduced to those who are assumed to have made no study of philosophy at all and there may be differences of opinion as to which of these methods is the best. This book attempts to define the fundamental issues of the subject, by giving some account of the historical theories, but the list of those selected is far from exhaustive. It is impossible to embody a comprehensive survey of the history of therapy in a book of modest compass.

There are many more philosophical concepts which can be adopted as suitable for individuals and societies. Probably, the most famous of all sayings being the Aristotelian 'know thyself', followed by 'moderation in everything'. 'Knowing yourself' is a good guide towards the understanding of human integration and the 'moderating factors' can be very useful to a human being. Aristotle also believed that happiness stems from human reason; ideal political state an enlightened monarchy. All his works have had a profound effect on thinkers throughout the ages.

Round about the same time the concept of 'moderation in all things' was urged by Epicurus. Epicurus was the founder of the term of 'hedonism'. He taught that pleasure is the chief aim of happy life.

In many therapeutic philosophical cases subjectivity dominates the client's catharsis, thus posing the questions 'Who am I? What is man?' Those familiar with Jean-Paul Sartre's and Albert Camus' works will recognise the concept of Existentialism. The client seeks to distinguish between essence and existence. Answers to such questions are many and can even conclude with the short comment of 'become committed to something, even yourself'. Sartre, as a leader of Existentialist movement, claimed that man creates a meaning for his existence by taking responsibility for own destiny.

Platonism can certainly hold its own in philosophy. Plato held that mankind often defeats the purpose of the Universe and its Creator. Further on, he maintained that it is man's duty to live a good life, but he may choose to live a wicked one. Plato was a student of Socrates and teacher of Aristotle, his teachings contained in written Dialogues. Plato, stressing the idea of the good rather than material appearances, has influenced the thought on therapeutic philosophy.

The French philosopher, August Comte put forward the thesis that mankind lived through major stages. The phase more interesting to the therapeutic philosopher is the 'final positive and scientific phase when he proceeds by experimental and objective observation, eventually to reach positive truth'.

Certain philosophical concepts, such as stoicism appear to be suitable to the modern one to one sessions. Stoics, the followers of Zeno, maintain that man should guide his life by reason and not by passion. Thus virtue was the greatest good. Stoics have also made a fundamental distinction between goals which are under human control and those which are not. In the second case, man must endure what cannot be altered while he cultivates the self-sufficient life of reason.

The concept of Utilitarianism by Bentham and Mill will be discussed further in this book. Basically, both thinkers

maintained that the greatest good of the greatest number is the criterion of morality, insisting that the real test of goodness was the social consequence.

This book attempts to define the nature and scope of philosophy generally and its application to the field of reasoning. The study of this chapter is essential at some stage if the logical foundations of philosophy are to be appreciated. Only so can philosophy in the proper sense be understood. For unless an examination of these logical foundations is undertaken, philosophy reduces, in effect, to science and never raises the essentially philosophical question of the extent to which the moral assumptions made by theories, can be rationally justified.

PURPOSE OF PHILOSOPHY

At the beginning of the twenty-first century, philosophy was regarded as a source of knowledge which transcended the discoveries of natural sciences. Science marked an advance on the uncritical and often unrelated beliefs of ordinary life, yet it was itself based on the observations of the senses and consisted of the uncertain generalisations based upon them; whereas philosophy was assumed to answer questions about such subjects as the existence of God, the nature of knowledge and the authority of the moral law upon which sense-experience, from its very nature, could throw no light. On such subjects, it was believed, reason was alone competent to pronounce and, when it did so, its conclusions were characterised by a logical and universal certainty, which the generalisations natural science could never claim.

That philosophical knowledge is certain and indubitable is a claim which all philosophers have made, or at least implied; that philosophical knowledge seeks to understand human nature. This is an unquestionable statement and as such this general agreement is reflected in the application of philosophy in therapy.

The different conceptions of philosophic counselling ultimately depend upon the nature of knowledge. The

propositions of mathematicians are usually cited as typical illustrations of such knowledge. For example, the proposition' 2 + 2 = 4' is said to be necessarily and universally true, on the ground that, once we have grasped its meaning, we recognise that it must be true. On the other hand, there are numerous propositions of which the falsity is perfectly conceivable. It may be true that 'a depressed person is withdrawn' or that neurosis is caused by bad early childhood experiences', but these propositions are not entirely true. On the contrary, there falsity is perfectly conceivable, even if observations appear to confirm their truth.

The discussion just illustrated is variably referred to as the distinction between rational and empirical knowledge, or between a priori and a posteriori knowledge, or between truths of reason and truths of fact. It is true to say that therapeutic philosophers claim, or at least imply that their theories are rational and a priori. Where one cannot differ is the view of the scope of such knowledge in therapeutic philosophy. The main difference has been where the view is held that rational knowledge is always analytic, while some have held the opinion that it is sometimes synthetic.

Those thinkers, who wish to expand on the knowledge of analytic and synthetic propositions, will find Kant's definition very useful. Immanuel Kant's definition is as follows:

Analytic propositions 'add nothing through the predicate to the concept of the subject, but merely break it up into those constituent concepts that have all along been thought in it, although confusedly', while synthetic judgements 'add to the concept of the subject a predicate which has not been in any wise thought in it, and which no analysis could possibly extract from it'. The difference is, in short, that the predicate in an analytic proposition is contained within the meaning of the subject, while in a synthetic proposition the predicate is not contained within the meaning of the subject, but adds something related to it. Kant illustrated the difference by the two propositions 'all bodies are extended' and 'all bodies are heavy'. The former, he thought, is analytic, because the concept of 'extension' is part of the meaning of 'body', while the latter is synthetic because the concept of 'heaviness' is not part of the meaning of 'body', but only a quantity which it acquires when it is placed in a gravitational field.

Kant's definition drew attention to an important difference between analytic and synthetic propositions, although not all analytic propositions naturally fall into the simple subject - predicate form which his examples illustrate. The essential characteristic of an analytic proposition is that it defines the meaning, or part of the meaning, of its subject and does not

describe unessential features which may, or may not, belong to it.

Modern philosophers have devoted much attention to the study of analytic propositions and have concluded that they do not make any assertion about the empirical world. They simply record our determination to use words in a certain fashion. They are, in other words, tautologies; and the reason why we think it worth while to assert them and sometimes, as in mathematics, to draw elaborate deductions from them, is that our reason is too limited to recognise their full significance without going through these complex verbal processes.

These considerations may appear to be extremely abstract and their connection with what is commonly understood as 'philosophic counselling' far from obvious; but in fact this connection is both simple and fundamental. For philosophy is the quest for certainty and if certainty is a characteristic of propositions, then an enquiry into the nature and scope of certain (a priori) propositions must be the essential task of therapy. If the general object of philosophy is to discover the nature and implications of rational thinking, then an enquiry into the nature of the propositions by which rational thinking is expressed is necessarily one of the most important tasks of therapy so understood.

All philosophers who have recognised the distinction between analytic and synthetic propositions agree that analytic propositions are necessary. Controversy has centred on the question whether synthetic propositions may also sometimes be *a priori.* The different answers given to this question have determined very different conceptions of the scope and purpose of philosophy. For if the propositions of philosophy must always be *a priori*, and *a priori* propositions must always be analytic, it follows that the propositions of philosophy must always be analytic.

Thus, if *a priori* propositions are always analytic, philosophy will be unable to demonstrate the truth of any proposition about the existing world except in so far as it is logically implied by an existential proposition whose truth has been established by empirical observation. The function of philosophy, in other worlds, will be to examine the implications of propositions and not to demonstrate their truth.

Until recently, it was widely believed that philosophic counselling could establish facts about the existing world quite independently of experience. Therapy was, indeed, often looked to for rational justification of beliefs, such as religious and moral beliefs, already held on non-rational grounds and

it was assumed that this justification could be given independently of experience.

During the present era, there has been a strong reaction from these methods and a growing acceptance of the alternative view that the function of therapy is to clarify rather than to extend the content of human knowledge.

The theory that *a priori* thinking can never by itself establish a truth about the existing world is known as Empiricism, since it always asserts that such propositions can be established only by empirical observation. The alternative theory that a priori thinking can by itself establish truths about the existing world is known as Rationalism. It is clear from the preceding discussion that Rationalism can be defended only if synthetic *a priori* propositions are possible. For if such propositions are not possible no proposition about the existing world can be established a priori, and some form of Empiricism must therefore be accepted.

RATIONALISM OF HEGEL AND KANT

Hume's revolutionary account of the function of reason naturally evoked a reaction, and the philosophies of the great thinkers Immanuel Kant (1724-1804) and Georg Wilhehn Friedrich Hegel (1770-183I) were attempts to restore to reason the positive functions which Hume had denied to it.

Kant and Hegel sought to do this by stressing the active function of the mind in knowledge and, in particular, by arguing that, while synthetic propositions may by themselves be devoid of logical necessity, they are characterised by another kind of necessity (which Kant called transcendental necessity') derived from the mind in which they originate. They are necessary, not in the logical sense that their falsity is inconceivable, but in the transcendental sense that experience could not take the form which it does take unless they were assumed to be universally true. Such, in brief, is Kant's theory of the nature of causal and moral laws. He admits that they are synthetic but claims that they are none the less a priori in the

transcendental sense. His theory is 'idealist' in the sense that he holds the song of experience to be independent objects but our ideas of or judgements about objects. While he believes that there are independent objects he calls things-in-themselves' - he holds that these are necessarily unknowable except in the form of appearances conditioned by the way in which the mind, in view of its structure, is bound to apprehend them.

Many philosophers would question whether a theory of this sort constitutes any real answer to Hume's empiricism. They would question whether 'transcendental' necessity is more than the empirical regularity admitted by Hume - whether, for example, the fact that we always interpret our experience in regularities justifies the conclusion that we accept it in this way. It must, at least be admitted, that other philosophers who think like him have their experience in this way.

Apart from this general objection to Kant's theory, Hegel thought that it was vitiated by the fundamental contradiction of asserting, on the one hand, that all

knowing takes the form of judging and yet claiming that experience cannot be explained except on the assumption that there are things-in-themselves. As Hegel was quick to observe, these propositions are essentially contradictory; if it is impossible for us to have cognitive experience which does not take the form of judging, it is impossible for us to know or conceive of or make any consistent assertion about things-in-themselves, for in so doing we are interpreting them in accordance with the way in which our minds are bound to think. Things-in-themselves which are thought about and talked about cannot be things-in-themselves; they must be things as they appear to the thinker.

Hegel, therefore, arrived at the conclusion that Kant did not carry his argument far enough and that its logical implication is that cognitive experience consists exclusively of judgements.

POLITICAL PHILOSOPHY

The naive conception of political philosophy as a set of dogmatic axioms defining the rights and duties of the individual conceals the basic purpose of philosophy. For philosophy consists essentially in directing the process of thinking upon itself with a view to ascertaining what thought consists in, and what it can establish. To lay down moral dogmas about the rights and duties of human beings without first considering how far this is a rational process is the very antithesis of philosophy properly conceived.

In the light of the foregoing considerations, political philosophy may be briefly defined as the study of the nature and implications of rational thought. From this general study conclusions may be drawn about the implications of rational thought in specific fields, such as the moral and political, and these implications constitute moral

and therapeutic philosophy. If, as the empiricist believes, philosophy leads to the conclusion that the rational part of experience is much smaller than is commonly supposed, this is itself a rational proposition of the first importance.

The purpose of this book has been to indicate, in the most general and summary fashion, the logical and metaphysical background of therapeutic philosophy. Large issues have been touched on which could not be adequately discussed in less than a volume devoted to their special consideration. But, enough will have been said for the purpose of the present book if it has been made clear that Therapeutic Philosophy is not an independent subject but is intimately bound up with the great issues of logic and metaphysics.

HEGEL'S IDEALISM

Georg Wilhelm Friedrich Hegel (1770-1831) was born at Stuttgart and received his early education in the local grammar school. In the autumn of 1788 he proceeded to the University of Tubingen as a student of theology, but did not achieve any distinction. Subsequently, he worked for a time as a private tutor, first at Berne and later at Frankfort, where he was able to devote considerable time to study, and to work out the outlines of his general philosophy.

The death of his father in January 1799 gave him a modest inheritance, and he was able to give up his tutoring and go to Jena. There he became a close friend and collaborator of the philosopher Schelling, and was soon appointed to lecture at the University in an honorary capacity. In 1805 he was appointed to an extraordinary professorship at Jena, but he drew little money from the post, and had to look for other work when Napoleon's invasion in 1806 brought the life of the University to a standstill.

After working for a year as a newspaper editor he became Rector of the Aegidien-Gymnasilim in

Nuremberg, a post which he discharged with considerable success until August 1816. During the eight years which he spent at Nuremberg, Hegel had been working steadily at his philosophy, and the first two volumes of his Logic appeared in 1812. In 1816 he was appointed as a Professor of Philosophy at Heidelberg. In 1821, he published his theory of moral and political philosophy in the Philosophy of Right.

Hegel's fame spread far and wide during his tenure of the Chair at Berlin and a Hegelian school of disciples soon began to form. In 1830 he was made Rector of the University, and in 1831 he was decorated by Frederick William III. But the revolution of 1831 was a great shock to him, and he viewed the prospect of more democratic forms of government with deep anxiety. His whole philosophy was based on the principle that the state is more important and more real than the individual, and prescribes the ideals of individual conduct. Hegel was not, however, destined to witness the aftermath of the revolution, for he fell a victim to the cholera epidemic which attacked Europe in 1831,

and died, after one day's illness, on 14 November in that year.

Hegel's political theory has been variously referred to as an 'Idealist' or 'Metaphysical' or 'Philosophical' Theory of the State. Of these adjectives, the most specific and illuminating is 'Idealist', since it describes one of the characteristic features of the general philosophy upon which Hegel's political theory is based. The adjectives 'Metaphysical' and 'Philosophical' indicate that this political theory depends, in a particularly direct and obvious way, upon a general 'metaphysical' or 'philosophical' theory of the universe; and a brief outline of its essential features must first be given if the foundations of the political theory are to be properly appreciated.

IDEALISM

Hegel's Idealism is essentially the logical development of Kant's doctrine of the categories. Kant had been convinced that certain synthetic judgements - in particular, causal and moral judgements - are a priori, and had traced this a priori character to the operation of the categories in terms of which the mind was, in his view, bound to synthesise the raw material of its experience if that experience was to take a significant form.

The validity of the categories had therefore to be postulated as a necessary condition of significant experience. But in Kant's theory the categories were only the formal conditions of experience; its material conditions were constituted by unknowable things-in-themselves. Hegel rejected the notion of a thing-in-itself, which lies behind and does not enter into experience, on the ground that it is a self-contradictory notion; for it seemed to him obviously self-contradictory to speak of that which, by definition, cannot be known.

Hegel therefore concluded that the categories must constitute the material as well as the formal conditions of experience i.e. must determine both the raw material of experience and its relational characteristics. For if the matter of experience is not determined by something which lies outside experience it must be determined, like the form of experience, by the necessary pattern of experience itself. There can be no external realm of 'things' or 'facts' by which the judgements which constitute experience can be accounted for or their truth confirmed.

Indeed, the usual conception of truth as a sort of correspondence between judgement and reality must be replaced by a new conception according to which the truth of a judgement is defined in terms of its relationship to the only entities to which it can be related, namely other judgements.

Truth, according to this latter view, means coherence, i.e. a judgement is true in so far as it is consistent with other judgements, and more true the wider the range of judgements with which it is consistent. The only judgement which is wholly true is therefore a

judgement asserting everything about everything,' for only such a judgement embodies, and is thus consistent with, the numerous judgements which, viewed from a narrower perspective, appear to be in some measure inconsistent with each other.

Thus Hegel rejected the distinction commonly drawn between knowledge and reality. Knowledge is reality and reality is knowledge, for if the two were separate reality would be unknowable and knowledge would be illusory. Since this implies that reality could not be other than it is-for it embraces everything in space and time, in imagination and in conception-knowledge could not be other than it is, and the contradictions which exist at the level of finite experience must disappear when viewed from the universal perspective of the Absolute. Hence, in Hegel's famous words, the real is rational.

KNOWLEDGE AND REALITY

The basic difference between Hegel's Rationalism and Empiricism obviously lies in the denial of a 'reality' outside experience. The possibility of such a reality is denied on the ground that its assertion would be self-contradictory.

For, Hegel maintains, reality is necessarily part of experience in so far as any assertion whatsoever is made about it; and, if nothing is asserted about it, it does not in any intelligible sense exist. From this general premise the Coherence Theory of Truth necessarily follows; for if the truth of a judgement cannot be defined in terms of its relationship to that which is not a judgement, then its truth must be defined in terms of its relationship to another judgement or judgements.

It will be true in so far as it is consistent with other judgements assumed to be true, but the truth of these other judgements will in turn depend upon their relationship to yet other judgements, and so on ad infinitum.

Hegel denied that this process involves a 'vicious circle'; on the contrary, he maintained that if it were pushed to infinity by asserting every judgement which is consistent with every other judgement the result would be one coherent system of judgements which could not be other than it is, and which would thus constitute absolute and a priori truth or the Absolute, as he called it.

While it is in practice impossible for a finite mind to achieve this absolute coherence, it is possible, by applying the test of coherence to an ever widening sphere of experience, to approach more closely to it, and thus achieve a higher degree of truth.

This amounts to saying that the conception of thinking held by the earlier rationalists was fundamentally mistaken. According to them thinking is a process of linear inference from a priori premises by a priori inferences to a priori conclusions.

Hume had effectively refuted this theory by pointing out that, where the premises afford grounds for drawing valid conclusions about the nature of the experienced world, they must necessarily assume a

synthetic form and thus be without any a priori necessity themselves.

Kant tried to save something of the older Rationalism by arguing that the more important synthetic generalisations (such as the laws of causality and morality) are necessary in a transcendental, though not in a logical, sense, meaning that their necessity is a necessity of experience though not of logic.

It was, however, left to Hegel to recognise the full implications of Hume's analysis and, in particular, to recognise that since the truth of a synthetic proposition is never an inherent characteristic of such a proposition it must be determined by the relationship of that proposition to other propositions.

This, Hegel believed, is the only self-consistent conception of truth which can be applied to synthetic propositions, for any attempt to define their truth in terms of correspondence to 'facts' or other alleged features of reality' conceals within itself the very concept which is supposed to be defined.'

Hegel would have agreed that purely analytic propositions are, in a different sense, necessarily true,

namely in the sense of being tautologies; but he saw that human thinking cannot be reduced to the repetition of tautologies, and he set himself to show how thinking can be at once rational and constructive. This, as already observed, he claimed to do by giving truth a novel interpretation in terms of coherence, and by arguing that such an interpretation is the only one which can avoid some form of self-contradiction.

Hegel thus claimed to show how can be at once rational and fruitful by defining truth in ten of the logical relationship of propositions to one another and by portraying thinking as a process, not of linear inference, but of dialectical evolution.

He thought it obvious that the greater part of human thinking does not consist in the assertion of tautologies but in the opposition of thesis and antithesis, and the evolution of a synthesis which marks a genuine advance on the thesis, and does not merely assert it in-different language . . But he differed from empiricists like Hume in holding that, although such thinking is not tautologous, neither is it the completely irrational sequence with which they identified it.

On the contrary, he believed that the apparently contingent features of the history of thought would, if viewed as a whole by an infinite mind, appear as the partial revelation of a logically necessary whole - the Absolute.

Hegel's theory is therefore something of a compromise between the older type of Rationalism and Hume's Empiricism. Like the earlier rationalists, Hegel believed that 'the real is rational', but he agreed with the empiricists that its rationality is not apparent at the finite level of human experience, and that thinking does not start from self-evident and *a priori* premises.

The novelty of his theory lies in his contention that human experience can be made progressively less irrational by making it more comprehensive and coherent, and that beyond it there lies the unattainable ideal of an infinite experience from which the last vestige of irrationality would be removed. If, in other words, we knew everything about everything we should recognise that everything must be exactly as, it is.

Theory of Knowledge

Hegel's claim that human experience can be made progressively less irrational obviously requires the postulation of an 'Absolute' embodying absolute truth since otherwise there would be no standard by which to measure the relative truth of judgements made at the level of finite experience. Yet it is just this ultimate postulate which he fails to justify.

However comprehensive an experience may become there is no rational ground for saying that it could not have been otherwise. It may, indeed, be conceded that an infinite experience, in virtue of its infinite comprehension, must be coherent, but this does not rule out the possibility that it could take an indefinite number of different forms, and could therefore be completely coherent in an indefinite number of different ways.

In claiming that the whole truth about anything would be necessarily true Hegel is, in fact, asserting a purely analytic proposition. He is saying that, if the universe is defined as the object A possessing the characteristics X, Y, Z, etc., then the judgement that A is X is necessarily true; but this is obviously an analytic judgement of the form 'A-which-is-X-Y-Z etc. is X'.

Thus Hegel's theory that all truths would be recognised as necessarily true by an infinite mind is nothing more than an assertion of the truism that if the Absolute is defined as the whole truth about everything then it necessarily implies the partial truth about everything. But there is no categorical reason why the Absolute should be constituted as it is constituted.

For these reasons Hegel failed to provide a foundation for experience which is at once synthetic and necessary even at the level of infinite experience.

All he showed is that human thinking at the finite level does, in fact, follow a certain pattern and that this is explained by the fact that all thinking takes the hypothetical form familiar in the natural sciences, and proceeds by formulating progressively more comprehensive hypotheses to account for the more primitive judgements known as the 'facts of experience'. This, Hegel believed, was the real nature of all the philosophical systems which had preceded his; hence his famous dictum that 'philosophy is the history of philosophy'.

But he failed to show why the history of philosophy should have taken just the course which it has taken, or why the Absolute Spirit should have manifested itself in just the way that it has.

If the foregoing criticism of Hegel's theory is valid it is fatal to his whole system, for it is essential to the latter to maintain not only that the whole of experience implies any part of experience but that from any part of experience it is possible to proceed by dialectical thinking to the whole. This is what Hegel failed to establish.

In so far as his dialectical process extends beyond the limits of analytic inference it is a synthetic process which widens experience only in so far as it proceeds beyond what is necessarily implied on a priori grounds.

In so doing the dialectical process may constitute a useful and culminating account of how the Absolute is constituted, but it can never show how the Absolute must be constituted, and if it cannot do this it cannot provide any real alternative to Hume's Empiricism.

The fundamental inadequacy of Hegel's dialectical method for the task which he sets it to accomplish can be illustrated by an analysis of the very first triad in his deduction of the categories. These 'categories' are the most general characteristics which apply to the whole of reality, and the dialectical method can therefore be applied most plausibly to the deduction of their relationships. If this application is found to be invalid it will be safe to conclude that the method

cannot be used to deduce the truth about the more concrete and less general features of experience.

Now Hegel's first triad consists of Being as the thesis, Nothing as the antithesis, and Becoming as the synthesis. Hegel regards *Being* as the original thesis because it is the most general and universal characteristic of everything in experience. Everything in experience necessarily is in the most general sense of the word 'is'.

But, Hegel argues, something which merely 'is' without further specification would be nothing at all. Everything which 'is' must have some further determination - must, for example, be material or mental, animate or inanimate, and so on. Hence, he argues, mere *Being* would be the same as Nothing.

The synthesis of the opposition between *Being and Nothing is Becoming*. By this Hegel means that Being 'passes into' Nothing and Nothing, in turn, 'passes into' Being. Such 'passing into' is not, of course, a temporal but a logical process. What Hegel means is that the thought of 'Being' is identical with the thought of 'Nothing' and that the thought of 'Nothing' is identical with the thought of 'Being'.

The two categories are therefore at one and the same time identical and different, and the synthesis of the dialectical triad to which their opposition leads is called Becoming.

Becoming is the unity which contains within itself the difference found within the identity of Being and Nothing. Because it contains and preserves this difference it is a relatively concrete universal - in contrast to the abstract universals of traditional philosophy which specifically exclude what is not common to all the members of a class.

This initial triad of Hegel's dialectic introduces two of his most important and characteristic doctrines. In the first place, it shows that Hegel believed that even the most complete opposition-that of Being and Nothing is an underlying unity; and, in the second place, it introduces the important doctrine of the concrete universal, according to which universals of the most abstract character contain within themselves, and logically imply, the most specific characteristics of their concrete instances.

It is obvious that this doctrine of the concrete universal is the key to Hegel's whole philosophy, for if it is valid it implies that it is possible to deduce species from genus progressively until the most specific determinations of experience are reached. This is what Hegel claimed to do. But the very first triad illustrates though not so obviously as some later triads- the fallacy which vitiates the whole process.

It is true that Being is equivalent to Nothing in the sense that Being in itself has no specific determinations such as mental

being, physical being, animal being, etc.; but this could not be deduced from reflection upon Being unless we were already aware of some of the concrete manifestations of Being. It is only because we have already experienced some of these manifestations-that we can say that mere Being is not equivalent to any of them, i.e. is Nothing; but this is an analytic inference from concrete experience and not, as Hegel contends, a synthetic inference from mere Being.

Examination of any of the other triads in the dialectic would illustrate the same point, namely that in so far as Hegel's deductions proceed from the relatively abstract to the relatively concrete they are invalid unless the relatively concrete is already experienced as that which the relatively abstract characterises. We cannot infer that mere Being is equivalent to Nothing unless we already know that Being frequently characterises something; and what it characterises cannot be logically deduced from it.

MORAL AND STATE PHILOSOPHY

These conclusions have an important application in Hegel's philosophy, which is an attempt to use the dialectical process to demonstrate the comparative morality of different types of political institution.

If his logic can be defined as an exposition of the principle that 'the real is the rational', his political philosophy can be defined in corresponding terms as an exposition of the principle that 'the right is the rational'.

According to Hegel, the essence of moral conduct is found when the individual acts not in accordance with particular impulses and desires but in accordance with universal reason- the reason which is shared by all rational beings. Hence Hegel rejects as wholly false all forms of a Utilitarian Theory of the State on the ground that they find the ultimate sanction of policy in the desires and interests of individuals. According to Hegel the 'will of the state' represents the true will of the individual, and only in so far as the latter coincides with the former is the individual acting morally.

Thus Hegel draws a sharp distinction between Civil Society and the state. Civil Society is that form of political organisation which follows logically from the disruption of the family due to children growing up and becoming

independent persons. At that stage they become dependent for various necessities upon other people, and thus accept a form of organisation which embodies appropriate arrangements for mutual support.

But Hegel believes that no rational man can rest content with such a form of political organisation since it assumes that every individual is seeking his own personal ends and regarding others simply as means to these ends. He can only be finally content with the higher form of organisation, called the state, which expresses the rational will of every individual contained within it, and in serving which every individual therefore finds the realisation of his true will.

Thus Hegel, like Rousseau, finds the criterion of political morality in the general will of the state. He readily admits that some states may not be perfect and that it would be going too far to respect the authority of every ruler or government; but all contain at least an element of rationality in their fundamental purposes.

Thus Hegel comments:

'Although a state may be declared to violate right principles, and to be defective in various ways, it always contains the essential moments of its existence, if, that is to say, it belongs to the full-formed states of our own time... Evil can doubtless disfigure it in many ways, but the ugliest man, the criminal, the invalid, the cripple, are living men.'

These observations certainly answer the criticism that Hegel held the will of any state to be a good will. But they give no indication how we may discriminate between good states and bad ones. If the dialectic process were really able-as Hegel thought it was - to provide valid deductions of the more determinate from the less determinate, then it might be possible to deduce from the conception of the state more specific criteria of its rationality. But, for the reasons already given, such deduction does not appear to be possible, and the conception of the 'will of the state' is therefore just as open to arbitrary interpretation and practical abuse as it was in Rousseau's theory.

RATIONAL WILL

The truth is that Hegel is no more able than was Kant to give the good will 'content', i.e. specific objective, unless it is possible to deduce the more determinate from the less determinate. To say, as Hegel says, that the good will is the 'rational' and 'universal' will does not tell us what it wills unless it is possible to deduce from the concepts of 'rationality' and 'universality' the nature of the objectives at which the rational and universal will must aim.

This is impossible unless the dialectical deduction of the relatively determinate from the relatively indeterminate is possible. For the reasons set forth above, Hegel fails to show that such deduction is ever possible, and therefore his whole conception of morality is based on a fallacious assumption.

In particular, he fails to provide any criterion for distinguishing between good states and bad ones, and thus makes it possible for the most arbitrary acts of government to be justified as the 'will of the state'.

Hegel, like Rousseau, distinguished the 'general will' or the 'will of the state' both from the 'will of the majority' and from the 'will of all'-in fact, from any actual will. They did so because by the 'general will' they meant the 'rational will',

i.e. an ideal will which is not necessarily expressed by the will of the majority or, indeed, by any actual will at all.

But while it is easy to talk of such a will it is impossible to define its objectives in a way that is not purely arbitrary, just because a will which is not, in the end, the expression of irrational desire is not a will at all. In other words, the conception of a will which may be nobody's will is self-contradictory and cannot therefore constitute a rational basis for morality or politics.

Hegel therefore fails, as Hume would have said he must fail, to provide a rational basis for Morality and the State.

His dialectical triad of Abstract Right-Morality-Social Ethics can at most claim to be a description of different manifestations of the moral sentiment. It cannot be, as Hegel thought it was the progressive evolution of a more rational conception of morality, since morality from its very nature is not of a rational character.

Similarly, Hegel's conception of world history as the progressive revelation of the Absolute Idea does not exhibit any rational necessity. It is impossible for a finite mind to deduce the future from the present, and to say that it would be possible to do so if only we knew the Absolute Idea in its entirety is equivalent to the analytic proposition that if the whole of history takes such and such a form, then any

selected period of history necessarily takes a certain form. If history has, in fact, developed by a sort of dialectical process with sufficient regularity to justify a generalisation, that generalisation is an empirical and not a logical principle, for it is without any sort of logical necessity.

The final judgement on Hegel's philosophy must therefore be that, like Kant's philosophy, it fails to refute the Empiricism of Hume. In particular, it fails to establish that synthetic judgements can possess logical necessity. If it fails to do this it leaves the essential principles of Empiricism inviolate.

For Hegel's Coherence Theory of Truth is just an alternative way of stating the empiricist principle that the only basis for a synthetic generalisation is a 'fact', but that the generalisation so reached is devoid of rational necessity. There is no reason why the empiricist should not accept the Hegelian definition of the truth of such a generalisation in terms of its consistency with the less general propositions which are said to describe the 'facts' upon which it is based.

Where Hegel claimed to have advanced on the empiricist position was in showing that the ultimate and all-inclusive generalisation - the Absolute Idea - is true in an absolute and categorical sense since it is both based upon, and in rum implies, every judgement included in total experience. But this, as previously shown, is simply equivalent to the

tautology that if experience as a whole is constituted in a certain way, then every part of experience must be constituted in a certain way.

It does not eliminate the ultimate hypothesis that experience is constituted in just that way, nor, therefore, does it constitute any reason why experience as a whole should not have been differently constituted.

This conclusion does not, of course, imply that Hegel's philosophy was not a powerful stimulus to fruitful speculation in the historical and social sciences, or that the processes of thought and history which his dialectic claims to express do not have a considerable basis in fact. But it does imply that those illuminating generalisations, which appear to correlate, and in some sense 'explain', the movements of human thought and history, are just the 'natural beliefs' of Hume's Empiricism, and are completely devoid of the rational necessity inherent in analytic thinking.

Their application to reality is therefore of a hypothetical and not a categorical character, since it is conditional upon the assumption of their truth. If the mental processes which result in these generalisations are to be described as 'thought', then it is necessary to draw a sharp distinction between such 'thought' and the very different type of thought to be found in logic and mathematics.

The rational necessity inherent in the thing of logic and mathematics does not characterise the formulation of empirical generalisations, and Hegel's attempt to deduce the latter from an all - comprehensive and self-justifying generalisation must be pronounced a failure. In particular, he failed to provide a rational basis for the ultimate principles of morality, or for the doctrine that these principles are most perfectly expressed by the 'will of the state'.

The reader must bear in mind that, whatever the criticism, Hegel is the instigator of 'knowledge is reality and reality is knowledge'. As such, therapeutic philosophers must not forget the meaning of his argument. Those responsible for the preparation of the curricula regarding the education and the training of therapist must not forget that 'knowledge-reality' is applicable not only to the individual, but also to modern governments; the states and their leaders who are in search of methods to improve the living of the people.

SOCIAL PRACTICES

Through the ages man has been pre-occupied with moral standards, probably more than other philosophical concepts. Societies through their various stages of evolution varied the theme with distinct differences in their demands on standards. These codes of behaviour were influenced by religions and the dogmas of each regional culture. What is acceptable in one tribe may be a fatal error in another society.

These variations of morality place a big demand on political philosophers. Individuals from different cultures, social groups, of known and unknown social norms may occupy the philosopher's thinking; the significance of this being the understanding demanded of the political philosopher. A sophist would investigate the background, the beliefs, thoughts, religion and other circumstances which may constitute the personal philosophy of the client.

There is no doubt that to establish the appropriate method for the agreed upon political system is a time consuming exercise, for all concerned.

LINGUISTIC EXPRESSIONS

"Language is the dress of thought," said Samuel Johnson 200 years ago. The way we talk colours the way we think, and the way we think shapes the way we act. We are the unconscious prisoners of our language. Most of the time this matters little, but at times of change in culture or society, our inability to use new words to describe familiar things can hide the future from our eyes.

More positively, metaphors from other fields can help us to glimpse new possibilities in old scenes, just as they have helped scientists to think creatively about the things that they observe but cannot explain. "Relativity" was not a scientific word until Albert Einstein borrowed it to explain the oddities he saw in space.

The premise of this section of the book is that the complicated language of new schools of philosophy no longer works as well as it should in modern society. It no longer describes what a person really is. It suggests the wrong priorities, leads to inappropriate diagnosis and screens out new possibilities. The terminology used is confusing because it does not make clear the individual's personal philosophy. It is an affront to human behaviour in that it gives inadequate recognition to the people and their beliefs.

WORK RELATED PHILOSOPHY

First, however, we need a new language to release our thinking. It should be the language of polity (citizen). A public corporation has now to be regarded as a community not a piece of property, although a community created by a common purpose rather than a common place.

The language of philosophy is then more appropriate for describing it than the language of business. No one owns a community. Formal communities need constitutions, which recognise the rights of the different constituencies and which lay down the method of governance.

The core members of that community are more properly regarded as citizens than as employees or "human resources", citizens with responsibilities as well as rights.

Good businesses, some may say, already do this. It is only common sense to give proper recognition to those who work with you and for you. Customers are now everyone's central focus.

Corporate governance, too, is in vogue as a discussion topic. The signs that some businesses are thinking like this only reinforce the contention that the time has come to update our concept of the corporation, to bring it into line with current practice and, not least, to fill the missing link in our idea of

citizenship. For once, good practice can change bad language, rather than the other way round.

The law, in western countries, tends to follow best practice. The first step, therefore, towards a goal of giving legal status to the real company would be to change the practice of the best companies. That this is already happening should be an encouragement.

It needs to be reinforced, however, by the legitimacy that a proper theory of community and the mechanisms of citizenship would give it. We can even learn from the practices and the problems of countries where the concept of the corporation and the language are different.

It is dangerously xenophobic to believe that capitalism is the only model that works. Corporations ought to be regarded as communities, as sovereign states within states.

The key difference is that a community is something to which one belongs, while it, in turn, belongs to no-one. A community is responsible for its future to its members, not its investors, who are entitled only to those due rewards. A community needs a purpose beyond itself in order to give it cohesion and motion.

MODERN ORGANISATIONS AND PEOPLE

Democratic institutions seek to balance power. Typically, they separate the institutions of legislation, execution, and audit, or in political terms, the judiciary. The legislature is representative of the different constituencies or interest groups; the executive is accountable to the legislature but can and should also service it. The audit function needs to be an independent overseer of the executive and its workings, as well as a guardian of the agreed constitution.

With the notable exception of Britain, democracies have written constitutions that set down the common principles and purposes of the state, the methods of governance and the rights of interested parties. The new corporate model will have the same.

The operating units need to be represented in the legislature, or the policy-making body. At present in companies, this is done at the executive or management level. It should more properly be done at the board level where the main investors would also be represented. It is at this level that the different interest groups should be reconciled and the overall purpose of the corporation hammered out, for a compromise will always be required between the shorter-term needs of most

investors and the longer-term requirements of the company to invest in its own future.

Such a board would inevitably be large. That would not matter as long as its role was clear. That role is to debate and ultimately to approve or reject policy proposals from the executive, although proposals can also be put forward by other constituencies. It would meet less frequently than is the current practice because, under the new concept, the legislative and executive boards are separated although overlapping. The executive and audit functions of this corporate state would need no formal changes to current best-practice.

The audit function should be independent of the executive, reporting to an audit committee of the board made up of outside directors. This is now common in the better organisations. It needs to become standard in order to encourage the corporation to take a broader and longer view of its activities.

Citizens typically have the right of residence, of free speech, fair trial, and protection from unfair treatment. In every developed country, except Britain, these rights are guaranteed by a Bill of Rights. In most developed countries they are also entitled, as of right, to education and a minimum standard of living. The only really contentious item

here, for businesses, is that of residence. It is no longer practical to offer permanent residence that is lifetime employment to anyone.

The principle involved is that commitment follows commitment. Re-organisation has first to grant a form of citizenship before it can reasonably expect the responsibilities of citizenship from its people. Similarly, not all temporary immigrants can expect to be granted citizenship. They will have to earn their right to a corporate "green card" after a period of effective probation, in order to ensure that they are likely to be able to make a continuing contribution to this corporate society and are in tune with its values and priorities. Recruitment standards are the key to any effective policy of citizenship.

The more subtle but important change is the switch from being an employee or instrument to being a citizen, whose interests are intimately tied up with those of the corporation, or at least of one of its operating units. The board of the corporation is now accountable for the corporation and its future to all its citizens and interest groups, be they inside or outside the company.

Corporations are not, however, accidental communities of place. They are communities linked by a common purpose.

The definition of that purpose becomes increasingly important.

The enrichment of the shareholders, beyond the level necessary to keep their support, is unlikely to be sufficiently inspiring as an objective to all except a few at the top, whose rewards are often linked to the share price.

A larger and, if possible, a more noble cause is needed to keep the enthusiasm of the citizenry. This becomes the key challenge for the leadership under the community concept of the corporation. It is much easier, conceptually, to wrap it all up in a search for a "better bottom line".

This, however, only begs the question of what you do with the money. Money-machines motivate only the few insiders who get most of the money. Great businesses have a purpose beyond their own survival.

STOCK MARKET AND PEOPLE

The great fear in all this is that the investing public will lose interest and that the hope of personal financial gain, which is the driving force of capitalism, will wither and dies. If shareholders only get the dividend promised to them by the issuers of the shares, they are no more than bondholders or mortgage holders. Not so. There is nothing to prevent them buying and selling their stocks and shares in the hope that some will pay more for the ones that look safest or surest, much as they do now.

On the whole, investors are not buying dividends (which are usually minuscule compared with the market price), but prospects of capital gain. The only difference would be that they cannot vote to sell the company or to buy another. That is because they would not be citizens but non-resident outside agents. Exceptions could be made for significant holders of the equity, say over five per cent, who might be assumed to be fully involved in the long-term health and prospects of the community. Venture capitalists and

the entrepreneurs that we all need would therefore not be disenfranchised.

For understandable reasons, the investing community has always been opposed to the idea of non-voting shares. It reduces its power. More respectably, it argues that it makes companies too cosy, but that is because the voting shares are often held by a small, self-interested coterie. In the new language of polity the votes would be held by those with most to lose by bad performance - the workers and the major investors.

The stock market has always been largely a secondary market. This secondary market will continue as it always has, but it will not have a direct impact on the community, although the signals it gives out will contain important warnings or encouragement for the directors. It will be what it has always been, a casino. But, at long last, a casino without the power to affect the lives of the dice or the cards it is betting on.

CAPITALISM FOR THE INDIVIDUAL

Organisations will continue to be one of the major communities of society, although they may well be radically different in shape and structure. They must begin to take that responsibility seriously and to think of themselves as communities, for their own sake and for the sake of all who work for them. Because the better businesses are already heading this way, there is little doubt that community-thinking will lead to improved results as well as to a more decent capitalism.

In the not-so-distant past, the trade unions gathered more power unto themselves than was good for them or for the health of the communities where their members worked. Now it is the turn of the financial community to see its powers reduced. It will turn out to be for the good of all. It needs no laws to make it start happening; just the creation of two types of stock and the enfranchisement of the real assets of any business these days - the people who work in it.

MODERN TIMES

In reading through these chapters, the reader will find that through the centuries, philosophy as a subject contributed more than any other subject in the shaping of our lives, how we exist, and how we control our destiny. It is true though to say that on occasions, philosophy together the sciences (with all the technological discoveries, the theories of evolution and genetics, the space explorations) and the arts, have contributed to our defiance of nature.

Psychologist tried to explain the bad and the good experiences and how they shape the individual. Some therapists maintain that it is the bad points, rather than the glorious moments that are most influential in personality development - in building the behavioural characteristics.

The author prefers the explanation of the idealistic philosophers. Where anthropos to them is kalos - man is good. It is this good nature of man that constructed the states, the democracies, with all the liberties to explore the sciences and to think. Thus moving forward in a positive manner.

'Story telling' through the electronic modes can only assist in preparing for the twenty-first century. Computing and systems influenced our lives, only to speed and send further out the public stories of history, politics, and philosophy. Information technology has and will have a bigger role to play in the education of the non-privileged and all the races. The turn of the millennium can only benefit more people - thus helping the improvement of everything on this globe.

MANKIND'S NEW CHANCES.

Politicians, in their patriotic moods, will ensure that everybody and everything in the environment will improve. Politicians are human, too. They are not always the egocentric individuals that the mass media try to interpret. They have families and they want their children and future generations to live in harmony.

Therapeutic philosophy for the person, groups, society and the state (and the rest of the cosmos) will be well established in the new millennium. Problems will be understood and solutions will be easier to find. Therapeutic philosophy practitioners will integrate the knowledge gained from philosophy and the logic gained from the great thinkers.

Humanity has more than two and a half centuries of philosophy (as we know it from written books), which can be relied on - to take us safely into the next millennium. Neuroses, uncertainties, lack of confidence.., will always be part of human nature. Therapeutic philosophy with its vast thesaurus of assimilated knowledge will always assist in the harmonisation of people and the smooth running of the state.

PHILOSOPHY THROUGH THE AGES

Historically, there are records of philosophical thoughts going back eight and a half thousand years. Recent excavations in Cyprus and parts of the middle east, show constructions of people living in a civilised manner; where the gathering of big communities held discussions on morality and acceptable (or prohibitive) modes of integration within their legal and accepted state boundaries.

Recorded thoughts, literature, poetry, art, religious beliefs, mathematical theorems and astronomical observations exist, proving that through the ages and since the Phoenicians, there have been influences on how humanity ought to behave and values which contributed to the evolution of thinking and the building of states. Individual standards, social norms, and group deities helped with the setting up of laws within which the citizens found freedom.

People live in groups and humans choose to live in states, simply for what they can get out of society. Those who choose to live in solitude become recluse in monasteries and nunneries, or become thinkers in isolation high up in mountains. The remaining who wish to explore their interaction with others, integrate within the moral and legal demands of a government.

EMPIRES AND THEIR IMPACT

The Phoenicians, Assyrians, Egyptians, Hittites, Greeks, Romans and the Israelites brought influence on how we live, think and behave, probably more that any other known races.

In recent times, the biggest influence to occidental, oriental, and African countries - also, the smaller and unknown nations - came from the powerful European empires of Britain, Spain, France, and Portugal... The influence on thinking, believing, morality, language and the legal systems of the ancient, classical and modern powers on other peoples were not passed on peacefully.

The people of lesser wealth did not (willingly) identify themselves with the leaders of the powerful nations. Changes in their way of living were done by force, oppression, slavery, and exploitation. In doing so (for their own benefit), some European powers left a legacy for religion and some form of philosophical thinking.

It is universally acknowledged that the biggest influence came from the Hellenic states. The rest of Europe gained the lights of civilisation from the Greeks. Subsequently and based on the classical Greek civilisation, the rest of the Europeans spread the Grecian thoughts, in a diluted or in an altered

version of rationalism which suited their needs. It is an acceptable fact that the Greek race has established the foundations of a holistic scientific knowledge and education, more than any other nation. This influence subsequently spread as far as India and the rest of the known world. Obviously, the Greeks did not conquer the world with altruistic feelings and helping hands. Greece and all the states within Hellas were always poor. To sit back and think, to invent and to debate democratically, and to let their philosophers explore their logic, it meant that they had to exploit the material possessions of other races, or putting it more mildly, whenever necessary they had to trade with other people, or sell their know-how.

The Greeks, like many other powers, used strategic talents and polemic methods to obtain what they wanted in order to support their financial requirements back home. You cannot build a successful state unless you are prosperous. So for centuries the Greeks did just that. Even during the Roman occupation - with the leadership of Constantine The Great, they built the Eastern Roman

Empire - Byzantium and for a millennium they isolated themselves within their Orthodoxy. Their false feeling of superiority, their arrogance and their political isolation did not help; what with the Christian schism and the total separation away from the Catholics, the damage done by the Crusaders and subsequent Ottoman attacks, it made them kneel; the effect being their complete surrender and capitulation to the Turkish invaders. Thus, with the conquest of Constantinople, the glory that was Greece went down. With the Ottomans capturing Byzantium and the Greek islands, Greece has never recovered. It is ironic that Greece with all its philosophy and civilisation is in need of therapeutic philosophy, more that any other state in Europe. The other two poor nations of the European Union, namely the old empires of Spain and Portugal are on the way to economic and social improvement. With the loss of their identity, the modern Greeks are still struggling to find their lost cause.

RECENT DEVELOPMENTS

A similar route for conquering other peoples was followed by the British and other European-based Empires. The British literature scene, the poetry, academia as a whole and philosophy, together with their language have contributed to the rest of the world's thinking, more than any other modern state.

Writers and poets such as Chaucer, Shakespeare, Milton, Dickens, Shaw, Wordsworth, Coleridge, Byron, Bacon... (Only a handful of authors are mentioned here), together with all the British Philosophers, their writings, thoughts and concepts have become household names around the world. In earlier chapters of this book philosophers such as Hume, Burke, Mills, Locke, Hobbes, Bentham and their concepts on Utilitarianism, Rationalism, Conservatism, Socialism and Morality are extensively discussed.

The British have also influenced their colonies with the English language (which will continue to be universally influential in the new millennium), their parliamentary democracy, the legal system and of course the popular English sports; most of the ex-colonies play cricket and the rest of the world football. The Spanish and their

inquisition spread Catholicism whether the American natives wanted it or not. The remaining of the European empires, as a legacy, they left mainly their linguistic communication and various dialects.

Germany and Russia only managed to conquer other European countries. It must be mentioned that, although Russia neither did nor conquer any other nation beyond Eastern Europe, their political system has definitely made an impact on many third world countries. The Soviet brand of communism influenced many other populations - East, West, and African people. Although Leninism has failed, there are a few nations who still follow their own form of socialism. The Teutonic race has given us Kant, Hegel, Marx, Rudolph Steiner and their modern engineering know-how. The German contribution to philosophy goes well beyond the two big European-wide wars. Such works on Philosophy can only be admired.

INTERNATIONAL SCENE

The United States of America with all their material wealth, they have not yet made an important enough impact to match the philosophy of their European ancestors - the idealistic philosophy. On the psychotherapeutic scene, they certainly contributed enormously. Having followed the psycho-analytical concepts for a generation or more, they expanded alternative methods of therapy and psychology in general, through Skinner on behaviourism, Carl Rogers on Eclecticism, on the modern form of Counselling and similar academic and practical applications.

But, regarding philosophy - one can certainly accept that the American concept of consumerism has gone where no other materialism has gone before. It all started with cinematography and then with the active 'coca-

cola-lisation' of the rest of the world, together with the silicon influence on technology.

Politically, their intervention in the Latin American countries, Vietnam, Laos, Iraq and the ex-Yugoslavian states has done little to improve the individual and the state, as is philosophically understood. Ironically, within the circles of political philosophy, it is accepted that the backing of Kuwait and other Moslem nations happened because of the empty Texan oil wells and the strategic geographical positions of Asia Minor, and not for the benefit of the people residing inside the warring regions.

MODERN PHILOSOPHICAL IMPACT

Philosophically speaking, the U.S.A.'s impact on the rest of the world is minimal in comparison with what the European philosophers have established. The U.S.A has been very successful in spreading the 'philosophy' of consumerism and the capitalistic freedom of trading. In an egoistic way, this is where the U.S.A. has excelled. With their vast natural resources and their technological success, the Americans will, for another generation or so, continue to influence the international political conflicts.

The existing political scene, through the United Nations Organisation, is influenced by the U.S.A. (more so now, because of the collapse of the Soviet block). But, with the re-formation and unification of Europe, the political influence of the European Union will show improvement to their international relationships - thus benefiting the smaller nations, the third world countries and the Eastern European countries. Economically, the E.U. will co-operate even

more with the oriental, African and Latin American nations.

There are many other negotiated initiatives that the USA has taken, such as the Israeli-Arab conflicts. As yet, there is no solid progress. Certainly the U.S.A. initiative to resolve the long lasting Cypriot political conflict has reached a stale-mate. In any case, as this book is primarily interested in the influences of philosophy on the therapy of the individual and the state, apart from the Hollywood and the remaining of the consumerism type of philosophy which comes from America, it still remains to be seen how influential the Americans can be on the philosophy theme.

It is an undisputed fact that the Europeans cultures have established a philosophy which can be compassionate and therapeutic to the states around the world and the people living within their own chosen governments. It still remains to be seen what other impact the Americans can have on the rest of the world, philosophically speaking.

END

HEGEL ON IDEALISM, KNOWLEDGE & REALITY

INDEX OF CONTENTS

BIBLIOGRAPHY

2011 Politics, Organisations, Psychoanalysis, Poetry, Andreas Sofroniou, ISBN: 978-1-4467-2741-6

Plato's Epistemology, Andreas Sofroniou, ISBN: 978-1-4716-6584-4

Aristotle's Aetiology, Andreas Sofroniou, ISBN: 978-1-4716-7861-5

Moral Philosophy, from Hippocrates to the 21st Aeon, Andreas Sofroniiou, ISBN: 978-1-84753-463-7

Therapeutic Philosophy For The Individual And The State, Andreas Sofroniiou, ISBN: 978-1-4092-7586-2

Philosophic Counselling For People And Their Governments, Andreas Sofroniiou, ISBN: 978-1-4092-7400-1

Moral Philosophy, The Ethical Approach Through The Ages, Andreas Sofroniiou, ISBN: 978-1-4092-7703-3

Medical Ethics Through The Ages, Andreas Sofroniiou, ISBN: 978-1-4092- 7468-1

Ross, W.D., Plato's Theory of Ideas, Clarendon Press, Oxford, 1951

Wedberg, A.E.C., Plato's Philosophy of Mathematics, Stockholm, 1955

Plato's Epistemology and Related Logical Problems, Gwynneth Matthews, Humanities Press, ISBN: 391 00260 0, 1972.

www.ingramcontent.com/pod-product-compliance
Ingram Content Group UK Ltd.
Pitfield, Milton Keynes, MK11 3LW, UK
UKHW020234250726
13967UKWH00001B/368

9 781471 709548